Chris Llewellyn's poetry collections include *Fragments from the Fire: The Triangle Shirtwaist Company Fire of March 25, 1911*, and *Steam Dummy & Fragments from the Fire: Poems*. Her poems have also been published in journals and anthologies, including *Sixty Years of American Poetry*. Among her other publications are essays on Muriel Rukeyser and on labor poetry studies. She has received the Walt Whitman Award of the Academy of American Poets and a National Endowment for the Arts Fellowship. She earned her MFA in Creative Writing from Warren Wilson College. Her new, expanded edition of *Fragments from the Fire* is a collaborative work with scholar/sweatshop activist Michelle B. Gaffey. Llewellyn's *New and Selected Works* (forthcoming, 2016) includes companion pieces for poems by her sister, the late Ohio poet Elizabeth Ann James.

Michelle B. Gaffey was raised in a working-class community in northwestern Pennsylvania. A multiple award-winning educator, she currently teaches composition, literature, and critical reading at the college-level. She has presented widely at local, regional, and national conferences. Her writing has been published in *The Collagist*, *Florida English*, and *The New People*. She is a co-founder of the Pittsburgh Anti-Sweatshop Community Alliance, an affiliate of SweatFree Communities, and in 2011 she coordinated with the Battle of Homestead Foundation and Duquesne University's Center for Women's and Gender Studies to organize a week-long series of events in Pittsburgh, PA to commemorate the centennial of the Triangle Shirtwaist Fire. Michelle currently lives with her family in Northern Virginia.

Out of the records and reports...*Llewellyn has created a transcendent work of poetry. The linked lyrics, the recurrent images, and the use of fixed forms are the work of a gifted and experienced poet. Yet the technical facility never obscures the terror and indignation of the event; the indignation never obscures the human tragedy. A book for all levels of readers.*

... R. Whitman, *Choice Reviews*, American Library Association, 1987

Because so many of Llewellyn's poems are dramatic monologues, they come alive in performance, ensuring that the Fire remains a touchstone of cultural memory. I'm convinced that Fragments from the Fire *would make a marvelous teaching tool. Combining poems in intricate forms (sestina, cento, sonnet) with documentary photographs, Llewellyn's book could make this difficult chapter in our history come alive, encouraging students to play the parts of labor organizers, factory workers, and the captains of industry who neglected worker safety to maximize profit. As long as sweatshops exist, Llewellyn's book reminds us to fight for justice.*

... Karen Kovacik, professor of English at Indiana University,
Purdue University Indianapolis and 2011-2013 Poet Laureate of Indiana

I wish this fire and Chris's words were just remnants of the past, especially in an age where media attention focuses on the latest device, app, or gadget. We need this book as a reminder (although it is much more) of what workers face every day, all over the world—unsafe working conditions. Llewellyn's writing transforms newspaper copy into a stirring and lyrical reminder of the importance of mourning the dead, and fighting for the living. She shows the power of poetry.

... Janet Zandy, emerita professor of English at Rochester Institute
of Technology and author of the award winning book,
Hands: Physical Labor, Class, and Cultural Work

The value of this book is in its multiple applicability: as a writing model for various voices; as a study in American history; as a tragic example of unfair and unsafe labor practices; and as a study in characterization. The range of reader interests that the book serves is, of and by itself, sufficient justification for its continued publication and ready availability. The quality of the writing—and the originality of the idea—are equally important aspects of the work, ones that should assure its continued acceptance and use in high school and college classroom and libraries.

... Martin Galvin, instructor of creative writing and poetry
at the Writer's Center in Bethesda, MD

Fragments from the Fire

THE TRIANGLE SHIRTWAIST COMPANY FIRE
OF MARCH 25, 1911

REVISED POEMS AND POETICS STATEMENT BY CHRIS LLEWELLYN

EDITED WITH ESSAYS BY MICHELLE B. GAFFEY

published by

Skye's The Limit Publishing & Public Relations, LLC
U.S.A.

Fragments from the Fire: The Triangle Shirtwaist Company Fire of March 25, 1911. © 2016 by Chris Llewellyn. All rights reserved.

30th Anniversary Edition - 1986 Walt Whitman Award

Published by *Skye's The Limit Publishing & Public Relations, LLC.*

Books published by Skye's The Limit Publishing & Public Relations, LLC may be available at special discounts for bulk purchases in the United States by corporations, institutions, and other organizations. For more information, please contact the Marketing Department at Skye's The Limit Publishing & Public Relations, P.O. Box 133, Galena, Ohio 43021, or via e-mail at talk2stl@gmail.com.

Cover background photo provided by the Kheel Center, Cornell University. Photo ID: 5780-087pb1f5c Fire fighters struggle to extinguish the burning Asch Building. Photographer: unknown, March 25, 1911. Back cover photograph courtesy of Florence Leebov.

Skye's the Limit Publishing & Public Relations
PO Box 133, Galena, Ohio 43021
talk2stl@gmail.com
skyesthelimitpublishing.blogspot.com

Published in the United States of America.

Paperback:

ISBN-13: 978-1-939044-03-7

ISBN-10: 1-939044-03-0

Website: FragmentsFromTheFire.blogspot.com

First edition 1987 Library of Congress Control Number: https://lccn.loc.gov/86015772

First edition ISBN-13: 978-0140585865; ISBN-10: 0140585869 (out of print)

20161230-2

PUBLISHER'S NOTE

CREDITS:

"The Great Divide" and "Ninth Floor Reprise" in *Building Blocks*, National Center for Urban Ethnic Affairs; "March 25, 1911" in *The Washington Review*; "Twenty-Sixth Street Pier," "At Rest in Green Woods" and "Potter's Field" in *Quindaro*; "Funeral for the Nameless" in *The Chester H. Jones Foundation National Poetry Competition Winners 1983*; "White Light" in *Talkin' Union*; "Stitcher" in *13th Moon*; "Sear" in *Evidence of Community*, Center for Washington Area Studies; "Triangle Site" in *Working Culture*.

"The Day When Mountains Moved" by Yosano Akiko appeared in the December 31, 1970 edition of the American periodical *off our backs*. It is reprinted here with permission of the Off Our Backs Collective, http://www.offourbacks.org. The poem was first published in Japanese in September 1911 on the front page of the first edition of the magazine *Seitō*.

Photographs on cover and pages 11 and 30 are courtesy of the ILGWU Archives, ILR School, Kheel Center, Cornell University.

Photographs on pages 17, 32, 41, 46, and 53 are courtesy of the Library of Congress.

Photograph on back cover and page 35 is courtesy of Ms. Florence Leebov, Pittsburgh, PA.

Photograph on page 22 is courtesy of Brown Brothers, Inc.

Photograph of Chris Llewellyn is courtesy of Julie Wiatt.

Photograph of Michelle B. Gaffey is courtesy of Robert R. Shuttleworth, Jr.

Contents

Poems concerning the Triangle Fire
of March 25, 1911, are written
in memory of sisters who died in the
Fire—Bettina and Frances Maiale,
Rosaria and Lucia Maltese,
Teresina and Sarafina Saracino,
Maria Lauletti and Isabella Tortorella—
and are dedicated to my sisters,
Sara Jane Reinhart and Elizabeth Ann James.

ACKNOWLEDGEMENTS

Chris Llewellyn was the winner of the Walt Whitman Award for 1986, sponsored by the Academy of American Poets. Judge for 1986: Maxine Kumin.

This is a revised edition of that book which was originally published by Viking Press in 1987 and again in *Steam Dummy & Fragments from the Fire* by Bottom Dog Press in 1993.

Special thanks is due to the late Leon Stein, author of the first book written exclusively on this tragic event, and to the ILR School's Kheel Center at Cornell University for their online exhibit of primary sources about the fire.

The poet also wishes to thank the District of Columbia Arts and Humanities Commission for a 1984 grant which funded technical assistance for the manuscript and to acknowledge the continued support of the Capitol Hill Poetry Group, the Jennie McKean Moore Writing Program, and the Festival of Poets and Poetry at St. Mary's College of Maryland.

One final note of thanks is due to Sarah Grey of Grey Editing, L.L.C., who provided invaluable editorial suggestions on the concluding "Historical Contexts" essay of this book.

Editor's Note

This new edition of Chris Llewellyn's *Fragments from the Fire* has been published to commemorate the Triangle Shirtwaist Company fire of March 25, 1911, one of the deadliest industrial disasters in New York City's history. One hundred years after this fire, in March 2011, thousands of people gathered across the country to honor the 146 garment workers who died at Triangle. In New York City, a fire department bell tolled as each victim's name was read aloud—the first time in a century that all of the workers who perished in the fire were identified by name.

Many of the commemorative events around the country featured rallies, speeches, music, art, and—not surprisingly—readings from earlier editions of Llewellyn's *Fragments*. Critical to the West Coast centenary events, for example, was the publication of *Walking through the River of Fire*, an anthology featuring "fire poems," including those from *Fragments*. In Washington, D.C., the American Federation of State, County, and Municipal Workers invited Llewellyn to read from *Fragments* for the memorial event at the Library of Congress, which was open to the community at large. Llewellyn's poems were also dramatically staged and performed for the commemoration ceremony in Pittsburgh, PA, which was collaboratively organized for the public by labor leaders and graduate students. *Fragments from the Fire*, a remarkable polyvocal book of poems, continues to speak to the deplorable working conditions that characterize the garment industry in this new millennium as it re-imagines the Triangle Fire of 1911.

Like the 1987 and 1993 publications of *Fragments from the Fire*, this 2016 edition expresses solidarity with the workers who died at Triangle and inscribes memories about the fire, its cultural context, and the social and political significance of its aftermath. This latest edition, however, offers contemporary audiences a new reading experience: the poet has revised select poems and has included new materials based on careful review of documents that have become available since the initial publication of her book. These revisions and additions reflect the poet's continued and renewed attention to the book's structure, to historical information and emotional truth, and to her contributions to contemporary conversations about poetics.

Readers of this edition will notice, for instance, that select scriptural passages are now clearly highlighted as epigraphic section dividers throughout the book, and the final poem—Yosano Akiko's "The Day When Mountains Moved"—is newly introduced with an excerpt from the book of Joel. The 1910 photo of "Shirtwaist Strikers, New York," which calls to mind the "Uprising of the 20,000," now immediately follows the poem "White Light" in which the speaker explains why "it's not easy to teach [garment girls] union."

The author has also chosen to modify several poems to achieve greater historical accuracy: some of the names of victims have been revised throughout the book, namely in "Scraps," "Four from Sonia," "Survivor's Cento," and "Sear," to reflect the spellings on documents that are now available through the ILR School's Kheel Center at Cornell University. Too, the poem "At Rest in Greenwood" is now titled, "At Rest in Green Woods," a subtle shift to indicate that the final resting place of the poem's speaker, Jennie Franco, is not in Greenwood Cemetery, as the original title would suggest (in fact, she is buried in New York City's Calvary Cemetery). Importantly, the space between the words "green" and "woods" offers this corrective as it honors the poem's publication history and maintains the symbolism of the original title.

Further, the subject of the imagined limerick in "Scraps" has been changed from "Joseph Asch" to "Max Blanck." While culpable for the loss of life in the Triangle Fire, Asch was the owner of the *building* that housed the Triangle Shirtwaist Company, whereas Max Blanck was one of the owners of the *company*. Garment workers would have been more likely to refer to Blanck as the "cruel boss," rather than Asch, since Blanck and his business partner Isaac Harris were known pejoratively throughout the industry as the "Shirtwaist Kings."

The first stanza of "Jury of Peers" has also been revised to include the names of all twelve jurors who served at the trial of Isaac Harris and Max Blanck, and immediately following this poem we now view Florence Leebov's striking photograph, "Garment Girls, June 1911," which had been removed from the text of the 1993 edition. Further, multiple lines of the second verse of "Potter's Field" have been modified based on the author's review of the transcript of *People v. Harris and Blanck*, though the details of Thomas Horton's heroic story, poetically re-imagined in this poem, still remain elusive to this day.

The author has elected to include two additional photographs in this new edition. An image of the "empty hearse, mountain of blossoms" from the funeral procession for the unnamed fire victims now precedes the poem, "Funeral for the Nameless." Further, a photograph of garment workers posing for a portrait, arms and hands clutching each other tightly, now follows Llewellyn's frequently-anthologized "March 25, 1911." This poem dramatizes the final moments of two Triangle Fire victims, Della Costello and Sophie Salemi, whose story was originally told in prose form in Leon Stein's ground-breaking book from 1962, *The Triangle Fire*. We wish to clarify, however, that the identity of "Della Costello" is most likely Giuseppina "Josie" Del Castillo, who, in 1911, lived near Santina "Sophie" Salemi on Cherry Street. Too, the final period of this poem has been removed to highlight the political and spiritual weight of the garment girls' martyrdom.

This new edition concludes with two supplemental essays. The first, "Summoning the Shade: Poetry as Vocation, Advocation, and Evocation," has been gracefully authored by Llewellyn; originally published in a collection of essays about Muriel Rukeyser in 1999 and again in 2001, this essay serves as Llewellyn's statement of her own political/spiritual poetics of evocation and advocation. The second essay, "Sweatshops and Resistance in the 20th and 21st Centuries," accounts for the rise of the global sweatshop—and concerted action against sweatshop conditions—in the late twentieth century, when Llewellyn's poems were first published.

Finally, we encourage readers to consult and reflect upon the Coda to this edition, which includes a list of names and ages of all 146 victims of the Triangle Fire. This information is courtesy of the work of labor journalist and genealogist Michael Hirsch, who analyzed hundreds of historical records to prepare for the centennial commemoration in 2011. An interactive version of Hirsch's work is accessible through the Kheel Center's online exhibit at *trianglefire.ilr.cornell.edu*. Our hope is that the supplemental materials offered at the end of this edition support the teaching and study of *Fragments* and other labor poems, and that they inspire further research into the history of sweatshops and resistance in the US and abroad.

Fragments from the Fire, one of the finest poetic accounts of the Triangle Fire and its aftermath, continues to restore, transmit, and form working-class memories even in 2016, thirty years after it won the Walt Whitman Award in 1986. The life of and lives within this book invite us—working women, men, and young people—to recognize patterns of global economic injustice. They inspire us to stand in solidarity with one another as we struggle for better working conditions and encourage us to continue to share working-class memories—the tragedies, the victories, and the lessons learned—with new generations. In doing so, we form and inform an international working-class collective that has, and always has had, the power to awaken and move mountains.

AUTHOR'S NOTE

The Triangle Shirtwaist Company manufactured blouses for women and was located on the eighth, ninth, and tenth floors of the Asch Building, at the corner of Washington Place and Greene Street, in New York City's Washington Square.

The company employed up to 900 workers at a time, but on March 25, 1911, only about 500 were present. These were immigrants, most of whom could not speak the English language. Nearly all were female, primarily Russian or Italian, although twelve nationalities were known to be "on the books."

At about 4:45 p.m., just after pay envelopes had been distributed, a fire broke out. Not everyone was able to reach the elevators and stairways. On the ninth floor, because the bosses had kept the doors locked to keep out union organizers, workers were forced to jump from windows. One hundred forty-six people, some as young as fourteen, perished.

Fragments from the Fire:

The Triangle Shirtwaist Company Fire of March 25, 1911

To proclaim the acceptable year of the Lord;
to appoint unto them that mourn in Zion,
to give unto them beauty for ashes…
the garment of praise for the spirit
of heaviness.

—*Isaiah 61: 2, 3*

THE GREAT DIVIDE

Henry Street, Cherry Street, Hester Street:
the new world turns towards old Jerusalem.
Sunrays stream on the bearded father-singers
standing beside a hundred rag-stuffed windows.

Chant the "Havdallah," chant "The Great Divide."

They praise the Almighty for creating us a Sabbath
that cuts one day away from the fabric of the week.
Bent over Singers, their backs to factory windows,
women and children stitch into sunset.

Wait for the darkness, time for going home.

They piecework shirtwaists under the company sign—
the letters set in English, Hebrew, Italian:
"If you don't show up on Saturday or Sunday,
you've already been fired when it's Monday."

Chant the "Havdallah," chant "The Great Divide."

Still the sun drops, and the fathers pour
the ritual wine into a little platter.
Each strikes a sulphur-tip match, touches
the surface of the small wine lake.

Lights in the windows, dividing up the dark.

MARCH 25, 1911

It was Spring. It was Saturday.
Payday. For some it was Sabbath.
Soon it will be Easter. It was
approaching April, nearing Passover.
It was close to closing time.

The heads of trees budding
in Washington Square Park.
The sun a hot flywheel spinning
the earth's axle. The days long
enough for leaving in light.
     It was Spring.

America's sweethearts—the ladies—
stroll in shirtwaists of lawn and lace,
mimic Charles Dana Gibson's Girls.
They pose in finery cut from bolts of
flimsy and stitched by garment girls
on Wilcox & Gibbs and Singer machines.
     It was Saturday.

Up in the Asch Building
in the Triangle Shirtwaist Company
Rosie Glantz is singing "Every Little
Movement Has a Meaning All Its Own."
Fixing hair, arranging puffs and tendrils,
the other girls in the cloakroom join in:
"Let me call you 'Sweetheart,'
I'm in love with you."
     It was Payday.

Attar-of-roses, lily of the valley,
still they smell of machine oil
that soaks the motors and floors.
The barrels near the stairwell
could fill a thousand lamps.
     For some it was Sabbath.

Here at Triangle, Sophie Salemi
and Della Costello sew on Singers.
Neighbors from Cherry Street,
they piecework facing each other,
the oil pan hitting their knees.
Tomorrow sisters will nail flowers
on tenement doors.
        Soon it will be Easter.

The machine heads connecting the belts
to the flywheel to rotating axle
sing the Tarantella. Faster,
faster vibrate the needles, humming
faster the fashionable dance.
        It was approaching April.

Sophie and Della up on Ninth
piece sleeves, race the needle's pace
not knowing on Eighth, paper patterns
burn from the wire, fall on machines,
spark moths and pinwheels round the room.
Rockets push up cutting-tables.
        It was nearing Passover.

On Eighth, cutters throw pails of water
on the lawn of flame, and Louis,
holding the canvas hose, hollers:
"No pressure! Nothing coming!"
        It was close to closing time.

Down on Greene Street, Old Dominick
pushes his wheelbarrow, describes
"a big Puff" when windows popped,
glittering showers of glass.
        It was Spring.

Swords flaming, Pluto flies to Ninth.
Sophie and Della and dozens of others
jump on machine tables; the aisles jammed
With wicker workbaskets and chairs.
        It was Saturday.

Mrs. Yaller testified: "Some froze at
machines. Others were packed in the cloakroom
filled with smoke. I heard them yelling
in Yiddish or Italian, crying out
the names of their children."
    It was Payday.

Reporter Bill Shepherd is writing:
"I remember the great strike of last year,
these same girls demanding decent
working conditions."
    For some it was Sabbath.

Rosie runs to the stairway. The door,
Locked! The telephone, Dead! Piling red
ribbons, fire backs girls into windows.
They stand on sills, see the room
a smashed altar lamp, hear the
screaming novenas of flame.
    Soon it will be Easter.

Pleats of purple and gold wave,
incandescent filaments of lace snow
in shrapnel of needles and screws.
The blaze from molten bolts stains
glass, walls and lawns—on Cherry Street
sisters nail flowers on tenement doors.
    It was approaching April.

"I could see them falling,"
said Lena Goldman. "I was sweeping out
in front of my cafe. At first some thought
it was bolts of cloth—till they opened
with legs! I still see the day
it rained children. Yes,
    It was nearly Passover."

Sophie and Della stand on windowsill,
look out on the crazy quilt of town:
We will leave for our
block on Cherry Street,
leave these skeletons
leaning on machines,
the faces fixed on black
crucifix of cloakroom window.
    It was close to closing time.

The *Times* quotes Mr. Porter: "The Triangle
never had a fire drill—only three factories
in the city have. One man I pleaded
with replied, 'Let em burn. They're
a lot of cattle anyhow.'"
        It was Spring.

Sophie and Della stand on sill:
We will leave, our arms
around each other, our only
sweethearts. Piling red roses
two white hearses pull up
Cherry Street and the Children
of Mary Society march
in banners of prayers.
        It was Saturday.

Captain Henry was the first policeman to arrive:
"I saw dozens of girls hanging from sills.
Others, dresses on fire, leapt from the ledges."
        It was Payday.

Sophie and Della look on crazy quilt of town:
Fifty of our schoolmates
sing in procession
O Trinity of Blessed Light
Our Lady of Perpetual Help
Ave Maria, Ave Maria
Now and at the Hour
of the Tarantella.
        For some it was Sabbath.

Ordering the nets and ladders, Battalion
Chief Worth explains, "I didn't know
they would come down three and even four
together. Why, these little ones went
through life-nets, pavement and all."
        Soon it will be Easter.

Sophie and Della stand on windowsill:
Look, the flywheel sun sinks
in the west. In the Winter
Garden, Mr. Jolson springs
and bows in blackface.
        It was approaching April.

At the Metropolitan Opera
George M. Cohan struts "The Rose
of Tralee" to the rich trailing
in diamond-sackcloth, rending
green ashes of dollar bills.
            It was nearing Passover.

Sophie and Della stand on sill,
look down crazy quilt of town:
Intertwined comets we will stream
the nightmares of Owners
Joseph Asch
Max Blanck
Isaac Harris.
            It was close to closing time.

Our Bosses of the Locked
Doors of Sweetheart Contracts
who in puffs and tendrils
of silent telephones,
disconnected hoses, barred
shutters, fire escapes
dangling in perpetual no
help on earth in heaven.
            It was Spring.

The Lord is my Shepherd
green pastures still
waters anointest heads
with oil overflowing
preparest a table—now
our arms around each other
we thread the needle where
no rich man can go spinning
the earth's axle we are
leaving in light

O Lord my God, thou art very great!
Thou art clothed with honor and majesty,
who coverest thyself with
light as with a garment,
who stretchest out the heavens
like a curtain.

—Psalm 104: 1, 2

SCRAPS

Lena Goldman speaks of Sonia

Garment workers from Triangle always came to my cafe.
Each Saturday the boys and girls in groups, arm in arm
and laughing. You'd think after fourteen hours packing
and sewing they'd be ready to drop! But not on payday.

Sometimes Sonia sat alone scribbling on scraps.
With such hours at Triangle, five brothers at home,
where else to write? Her poems weren't Moon-June or
like that. At first she only wanted us to laugh.

There was a cruel boss named Max
who preferred his potatas mashed.
When the women talked union, he was thrashin
and stewin. Soft-in-the-head, Mr. Blanck.

Oh, she was a bright one! Serious poems too:
Tonight all over the world
garment girls are looking out
looking up at stars…

Seventeen years old and writing English!
Well, after the Fire, her father came in crying.
"Like losing her twice," he kept saying—
since Sonia's notebook burned up too.

He can't afford to educate his sons.
Yet even in better times, a daughter
wasn't sent to the House of Studies.
"But in America," Sonia said, "I will find my way."

FOUR FROM SONIA

Is the room swept, blankets
pressed and folded chairs
lined in readiness straight
oh hang the heavenly picture.

Writing poems with a cardboard
bookcase my only company
the poplar tree shifting shades
and whispering: remember me.

Boarding houses yes
lived in four or five or more.
Don't think I'll ever get
the smell of urine, frying
potatas and Evening in Paris
outa my head.

Going outside sunny sunny
rubbing leaves try to
out eclipse each other.

DEAR UNCLE STANISLAUS

March 18, 1911

      I pray this letter finds you in good health.
Coming over, a great storm. Water came down the ship
chimneys. Eight drowned. Thanks to Our Lady, I survive.

      Uncle, do not believe gold lies in the street.
This is no golden land. Still I have work enough with
bread and meat to eat.

      Such noise in this nation! All hours people shout.
Always factory bells and whistles. Up in the loft the
clatter of cloth in machines.

      Uncle, write. Tell me, did the potatoes freeze
this Winter? If so, what was to eat? Could you sell
the wheat?

      Next to Triangle Waist is a park with flowers and
birds. But who has time to enjoy? Who will pay for
that? Soon it will be Easter and at last a holiday.

      They say with everyone coming here, Europe will soon
be empty. Next payday I am sending money. Give my love to
Auntie but save the large part for yourself.

Love,
Marie

P.S. Uncle, did our storks come back this Spring?

CUTTER AND MOTHER

1.
Each morning children squeezed
inside a wire cage that pierced
the pit at extreme speed. *SLAM.*

At six, my mother went to the colliery
alongside her cousins and brothers.
Foremen liked them thin and short

For dynamiting narrow tunnels.
She recalls tall ones were trappers
waiting alone for the rolling-down

Black shaft and only a split-second
to jump aside, open-shut trap door.
She's proud none of her sons spend

Daylight crawling into darkness.
Not harnessed and roped like pit
ponies. No. Not one.

2.
Before first shaft of morning
I put bread and cheese in my sleeve,
race down to Triangle Shirtwaist.

My knife cuts away from daylight,
carves layers round the paper patterns.
Sleeves, collars, flaps; white scraps

Fall to the floor. Pile up dove-tails,
wings, eight stories over the streets
and tunnels. But Mother what about

Parts deep inside me, what you can't
see with your eyes. For twelve hours
not a soft word spoken. Machines scream

For more cloth, faster, more cloth.
And at night, to fall exhausted into
dreams that bring no music or painted

Pictures. Mother even the pit pony
that is beaten gets a sweet to eat
pat on her head once in a while.

IMAGINING THE HORSE

Captain Meehan's horse, Yale,
was the first to arrive on the scene.

My name is Yale. At first
Hail of cinders.
Glass. Fire bells.
Falling bales and
timbers. Blood-smell.

Then:
Tarp-covered mounds.
Waterfalls from windows.
Hoses tangled in bundles.
Gutters red to fetlocks.

Night:
Searchlight.
Block and tackle.
Gray men in lines.
Stacks on wagons.

Journey:
Slow pull up Broadway
to Fourteenth to Fourth Avenue to
Twenty-third. Clanging. Wailing.
Twenty-sixth Street Pier.

Dawn:
The Sun has dropped
her mares and foals.
Plentiful as flies.
Wrapped in rows.

TWENTY-SIXTH STREET PIER

A temporary morgue

1.   Half-past midnight, a hailstorm
broke, smashing in the roof glass.
Arc lights spun and sputtered,
rain and hail fell on faces in rows.
Policemen swung their lanterns low,
picked out the glass, copied down
numbers from the caskets.

2.   I tell ya, folks here still
call the pier "Misery Lane."
Not so long ago you'd see
the blind and insane
beggars and homeless-old
boarding for the poorhouse
or the T.B. hospital.

      Boats off to bedlam
or the penitentiary.
Landing them forever
on the islands
in the river.

3.   A double line of winos lifted
the bodies, followed the carts
to the Twenty-sixth Street Pier.

      Mornings when the families came
panhandlers poured them coffee,
held up the fainting.

      You can always get derelicts
to do the dirty work.

4.   *A derelict speaks*

      Opium dives, canned-heat alleys
a night in the can's better than
coppers and corpses. I'd rather
the dry-heaves from dogcheap rotgut
or the DTs than seeing brothers
search for their sisters or
mothers calling their sons.

MERCER STREET PRECINCT REPORT

1.
One gent's watchcase
one man's garter
one razor strop.

One-half dozen postcards
one yellow metal ring
one one-dollar bill.

One lady's purse with rosary
one small mirror
one pin with painted picture.

2.
One pin with painted picture

Earthwork windmill rises, boxed arms
tilted to white heavens. Then little
wood sticks stalk garden walk.

Birds weaving cumulus dive to tulips
named for wishes: Yellow Moonstruck,
Windsor Castle, Tender Shepherd.

Inside shuttered cottage walls,
Kit and Kat lick whiskers, purr
by fire. Kettle spurts water.

THE FOLLOWING

Sure as smoke follows flame they came:
"Souvenirs from Triangle! Rosaries! Earrings!
Get your machinist's cap—or laces from his boots!
Hair ribbons from a dead girl's head!"

Sure as fish brings flies. Rabbi warned us
"Schnorrers"—solicitors for phony "funeral funds"—
would come when all along it was the Hebrew Free Burial
that was paying. "Sure as flood brings mud," he said.

A few from the Social Register ordered chauffeurs
to drive directly to police lines, demand they
be let through, so as to view this "spectacle."
Sure as carrion brings buzzards.

Ladies in lace shirtwaists, gentlemen in frock-coats
out for a Sunday stroll, filed up Fifth Avenue,
caught the stage-buses to the Twenty-sixth Street Pier.
High-hats in the long lines leading to the dead!

"I AM APPALLED"

New York Governor Dix

The Police commissioner
gripes to the Mayor who points at
the Governor, "I am appalled,"
who sets on the State Labor Commissioner
who blames the National Fire Underwriters
who turn on the Fire Commissioner
who cites the "City Beautiful"
(for finding fire escapes ugly)
who then faults the Architects
who place it on Tenement Housing
who says failure of the Health Department
who then proclaim conspiracy
between the Utility Companies and
the Police Commissioner.

I made sackcloth also my garment;
and I became a proverb to them.

—*Psalm 69:11*

AT REST IN GREEN WOODS

Jennie Franco

My short years wrap me like a cloth
of schooldays, feast days, my First Communion dress.
The cord of mornings, stitching at Triangle
up in the loft before light.

I trace the thread to my last, my fifteenth birthday.
Ribbons of friends dance the Tarantella,
circling plates of tortoni and ices
out on our stoop after dark.

And Mama says, don't forget Our Lady
and always light a holy candle on your birthday.
Today she twists rosary beads between my ruined fingers,
plaits roses in my veil.

Neighbors nail flowers, black crepe
to the doors, they have covered my face
with lilies and forget-me-nots.
I am circled with tapers.

I rest in the front room
next to the room where I was born.
The brass band wraps up our street,
"Panis Angelicus" stops at our stoop.

The Sons of Italy and Saint Angelo Society
have hired a cart just for my flowers.
Papa says, only the best for our Jennie.
A fine lady. I am lifted into my carriage.

The brass-harp of hymns follows the line
of Eleventh Street. Inside its woven voice
I know each murmuring Ave Maria.
The sky smells like lilies.

Slower. Silence. We are nearing Triangle.
Now the shock of the skeleton loft
unfolds the tall wall of wailing till
Heaven cracks and tatters, blesses us with rain.

FUNERAL FOR THE NAMELESS

Rose Schneiderman speaks

For miles the bereaved stream
under a single banner:
"We Demand Fire Protection."

The bunting's blue dye drips down
arms and faces of the honor guard,
eight of our youngest garment girls.

From the tops of tenements
bending out of windows
watching us.

Women, children, the old ones
lean on sashes, stare through
rain screen, down to deep street

Where white horses draped in black net
pull an empty hearse, mountain of blossoms.
As we march up Fifth Avenue

There they are on tops of hundreds of
buildings—structures no different from
the Asch Building and as for lacking

Fire protection, many much worse
than Triangle. It is this, not
cold rain, that makes me sick.

At each curb's turning, window-banks
empty of waving white handkerchiefs.
Thunder drums down the narrow stairways.

Thousands pour to Evergreens where over
the empty pits, rabbi, priest, preacher
bless the waiting coffins.

With holy water, hymns, their prayers
pronounce the placards' numerals:
46, 50, 61, 95, 103, 115, 127.

SURVIVOR'S CENTO

All through the day rain ever and again.
The quartet from the Elks Lodge sang "Abide with me."
They lost both daughters, Teresina and Sarafina.
Last year I was one of the pickets arrested and fined.
We were striking for open doors, better fire escapes.
Freida Velakowsky, Vincenza Bellota, Celia Eisenberg.
You knew the families from the flowers nailed to the doors.
That's my mama. Her name's Julia Rosen.
I know by her hair. I braid it every morning.
Now the same police who clubbed the strikers
keep the crowd from trampling on our bodies.
Sadie Nausbaum, Gussie Bierman, Anna Cohen, Israel Rosen.
I know that's my daughter, Sophie Salemi.
See that darn in her knee? Mended her stockings, yesterday.
Box one-twelve: female, black stockings, black shoes,
part of a skirt, a white petticoat, hair ribbons.
I would be a traitor to these poor burned bodies
if I came to talk good fellowship: Jennie Franco, Rosie Weiner
Julia Aberstein, Joseph Wilson, Michaelina Nicolosei.
I found a mouse on the ninth floor, took it home,
kept it for a pet. At least it was still alive.
Our children go to work in firetraps, come home and sleep
In firetraps. Day and night they are condemned.
Ninth floor looked like a kindergarten. We were eight,
nine, ten. If the Inspector came, they hid us in bins.
Rose Feibisch, Clotilde Terranova, Mary Leventhal.
That one's Catherine Maltese, and those, her daughters.
Lucia, she's twenty. Rosaria—she'd be fourteen.
Those two are sisters. Bettina and Frances Maiale. M-A-I-A-L-E.
We asked the Red Cross worker how to help
and she said bring books—Tolstoy, Shakespeare in Yiddish.
Benny Costello said he knew his sister Della by her new shoes.
Anna Ardito, Gussie Rosenfeld, Sarah Cooper, Essie Bernstein,
reminders to spend my life fighting these conditions. Antonina
Colleti, Daisy Lopez Fitze, Surka Brenman, Margaret Schwartz.
One coffin read: Becky Kessler, call for tomorrow.
The eighth casket had neither name nor number. It contained
fragments from the Fire, picked up but never claimed.

———————

Cento is a Latin word for a garment made of patches.

JURY OF PEERS

Morris Baum, sales.
Leo Abraham, real estate.
William Akerstrom, clerk.
Abraham Wechsler, secretary.
Joseph Jacobson, sales.
Arlington Boyce, management.
H. Houston Hierst, importer.
Harry Roeder, painter.
William Ryan, sales.
Victor Steinman, shirts.
Anton Scheuerman, cigars.
Charles Vetter, buyer.

Mister Hierst summarized:
I've listened to the witnesses
and my conscience is clear.
Harris and Blanck are pretty
good managers. We've reached
the decision that the type
of girl you have at Triangle
is basically less intelligent.
Hell, excuse me, Your Honor,

But most of em can't even read
or speak English—and the way
they live! They're lots
less intelligent than the
type of female you find
in other walks of life. I mean
that kinda worker is more—
well—susceptible to panic.
Emotional females can't

Keep a clear head they
panicked and jumped my
conscience is clearly
Act of Almighty
God they jumped
conclusion Your
Honor owners
of Triangle
not guilty.

The children which thou shalt have
after thou hast lost the others
shall say again in thy ears:
The place is too strait for me;
give place to me that
I may dwell.

—Isaiah 49: 20

GRAND STREET

After Sophie Ruskay

We lined the walks in chalk boxes, numbers.
Played potsy with markers of tin. Or spinning
tops, we'd only stop for the hokeypokey man who
sold a slap of ice cream on a piece of paper for
a penny. Papa complained potsy and dancing wore
shoe soles through in just two weeks and told us
not to leave our block. Still I skipped to

Grand Street to dream at the dolls in windows.
Each splendid in real silk and lace. Blue eyes,
golden hair. Their brass-bound trunks for travel
brimmed kidskin boots and fur-trimmed bonnets.
One mamselle in ashes-of-roses held a pink parasol.
At her feet, a white batiste shirtwaist was displayed.
The kind Mama made at Triangle. Back before the Fire.

WHITE LIGHT

After Sonya Levien

It's not easy to teach us union.
Garment girls shift like sand, start
too young in the trade, wait for

Prince Charming to take em away.
When I arrived from Russia
my cheeks like apples. And look now!

But talk about a dreaming fool!
Me, thirteen in the Golden Land
longing to work at Life and Love.

Be what you call a builder of bridges.
Yes, I'd go back, show all Moscow
a great American lady.

My first position: feeding kerchiefs
to machine. First English sentence:
"Watch your needle—three thousand stitches

A minute." Say, I was some swift kid
in those days: seventy-two hundred
an hour, eighty-six thousand pieces

A day, four dollars in the pay
envelope—and that the busy season.
For three months my pay was bread.

I yearned to earn wages, save my
little sister's passage, I was so
lonely in America. Soon like the rest
I grieved at my machine, swore I'd
marry any old man just to get out.
One by one the others left to marry

But returned to the shop. In them
I saw my future in a white heat light
no dreams could soften.

SHIRTWAIST TUCKER

Sadie Hershy

The Fire? That was
Nineteen-and-eleven.
Yes I was a garment girl
a tucker at Triangle.
We'd haul big bolts of cloth
feed em to pleating machines
that crimped the folds
at neck and wrists—
to take in fullness or
decorate the yoke.
Saturday was payday—
twelve dollars for sixty hours!
Oh I could make do
better than most though.
Winter was bitter
and prices dear.
Bit by bit bought me
a warm wool coat.
And in Spring
a white batiste waist.
Was a real American lady
come High Holy Days!
Say that was a slave-driving place.
Couldn't talk to your neighbors
and the bosses kept doors locked.
Looking out for organizers.
Agitators.
That afternoon I was close by
the cutting-table
spied a little snake of smoke.
So I says to the manager
"Mr. Bernstein I see smoke."
And when he tipped water from
a little wooden bucket
such a flame shot up!

POTTER'S FIELD

Thomas Horton speaks:

A few of us back then were porters in the district
bundling scraps under the cutting-table or
after the packers crated the shirtwaists—why,
we'd haul them on down to Washington Place.
My grammaw told me when she was a girl
Washington Park was a potter's field and used
to say the nameless passed to glory anyway.
Soon as the high-class built here, potter's field
became a park with bushes and benches,
a garden spot for their fancy townhouses.
(We laughed at how those homeless bones
were pushing up a monument to President Washington
who once sold a slave for a bolt of cotton cloth.)
Then the factories came and company housing—
tenements you call em. Crowded! You don't know
the word! But you want to hear about the Fire.

Well, once the cries of fire broke out, the shouts
and call bells came faster and faster until their sounds
rang nonstop and at one with screams and prayers
for help or hope. Somehow Gaspar and Giuseppe kept
that crammed car running while I stayed in the basement
tending the machines so cables wouldn't snap or
cabins crash into the pit. Because of smoke they
couldn't see the floors, had to open up the doors
by guesswork. Girl, we ran those cars till they
couldn't run no more, we kept putting in switch
cables till they ran with water and stuck.
Circuit breakers were blowing out all over the place.
The ladies were jumping on the cars, even slid
down the ropes—why there were twenty on the roof!
The ones that got inside grabbed at Gaspar's arm,
pulled his hair, jabbed his face. Christ A-mighty!
They were climbing down the cables!
That was the passenger car, you understand.
Though later the papers said a brave passerby
had raced into the choking smoke to operate
the freight elevator. Here I'd like to state
some of us porters—all Negroes—testified
at the trial. The headlines named Giuseppe
"Heroic Elevator Man."

STITCHER

For Judith Hall

It was soon after the Fire
I was employed as a housemaid.
Now I wash the garments and
some I starch. Stiff as grief

Or courage. That flat iron presses
and gives shine. In the morning
there are lamps to fill, globes
wiped so light can shine through.

Windows thrown open for sweeping
and dusting. Mid-days, Mistress
sometimes recites scriptures or
legends like Paramhansa the swan

Who could sup up milk, leave
water in the saucer. She says we
separate pure from impure in our
breathing, that new cells replace

The old. I know remade garments
bring fair material from that
judged hopeless and so my needle
joins torn places, mends worn parts.

Each stitch carries a blessing.
Don't you know handkerchiefs keep
secrets, that hat trims see hair
as a halo of the spirit, crown of Life?

A skillful housemaid will not pour
boiling water over flannel or use
strong soap on silk or organdy.

In the evenings, I've learned
the Language—alphabet, vocabulary,
grammar rote by gaslight sputter.

Tonight I write this history
into my copy book: Gehenna.
Gehenna, a word for garbage burning

Outside the walls of Jerusalem.
The refuse of the city. Corpses
of criminals, sacrificed animals.

Holocaust of relics, regrets, evil
memories released into smoke.

SACRISTAN

Before Mass, I fill silver cruets
with wine, water, place pressed linen
under pallboard, over chalice, lavabo.
The priest's vestments must be laid
just so—blue for Lady Day, purple
during Lent, white for first-class
feasts , green for ordinary, always

Red to commemorate the death
-dates of the martyrs. We study
the lives of Lawrence and St. Joan
and in a symbol book look up
their signs of stake and gridiron.
When the sanctuary lamp burns low
I'll trim the wick and fill the oil,

Trade candelabra stubs for tall,
taking care to pare beeswax drips
from the tops of golden holders.
Fresh charcoal, sandalwood incense
for the censor. And now to work
before the morning bell! Rags,
brushes, mops. Scrub and shine

Steps, pews, floor. Ora Labora.
Labora Ora. Prayer is labor,
labor the prayer. I polish and
pray the names of my brother,
of all the shirtwaist martyrs,
so these holy ones may intercede
for us on earth.

In my monastic breviary I mark
any mention of fire or garments
and collect those psalms into
my copy book. I've composed
a homily on the example
of the beekeeper who handles
her charges, yet is not stung.

NINTH FLOOR REPRISE

Fifty-eight girls crowded into a cloakroom.

The glass blackens and shatters.
Who will come for us?

Up on Tenth, typists and bookkeepers leave
ledgers to ashes, machines to melt.
The packers and switchboard-lady gone
the phone cords and crate slats spurt
split into stars and meteors.

Up on Tenth, our finished shirtwaists unfold,
crack the crates, jump upright, join sleeves,
dance the hora and mazurka, spin like dreidels.
They call to us, their makers:
Stitcher, Presser, Cutter, Tucker.

"I saw them piled," testified Fireman Wohl,
"they pressed their faces toward a little window."

Gather up the fragments that
remain, that nothing be lost.

—*John 6: 72*

STADIUM SESTINA

Remembering high school commencement
while researching the Triangle Fire of March 25, 1911

The poorest student—me—with the loudest voice reads the script:
"Mother of Exiles from her beacon-hand…"
Our town in the stadium bleachers looks down on circumstance.
In the east, the Triangle papers slowly rise on imperfect wings
of file folders, pamphlets, fly to this valley of newsprint
song sheets. Where are the words of fire for my generation?

Our parents and teachers became the first generation
after that of 1911, the year these martyrs taught History the script.
Their shredded alphabets of flames pierced the clouds of newsprint.
(Ashes are drifting seventy years to light on my left writer's hand.)
At Commencement, our graduation sleeves split in wings,
the orchestra strikes up Pomp and Circumstance.

The owners of Triangle profited from fires (all were created circumstance).
From Europe, Italy, Jamaica, Palestine, Russia—the immigrant generation
crossed to Ellis Island, bundles piled, shawls spread in wings.
Each wage-earner signed an "X" or Arabic-Cyrillic-Hebrew script.
On payday, March 25, 1911, no one knew how many were on hand—
the hired and fired, dispensable as newsprint.

The *Herald, Sun, Telegraph,* and *Times* set photos into newsprint,
hurried to interview witnesses, each tried to scoop the circumstance.
…Now Commencement ends. The principal shakes my hand,
pronounces: "We pass the torch to a new generation."
Every year the same old line ends the script.
Whether graduation or when our town's a tour-stop for the Wings

Over Jordan Choir—black angels singing God's chillen got shoes/ harps/ wings.
Since the time of Triangle, turpentine torches of rags and newsprint
were replaced by gas lamps, then by electric arc lights. So says the *Script
for the Centennial.* Citizens in beards and bonnets recreated the circumstance
and Miss Liberty raised her beacon flashlight beside golden generations
of post-Depression years. (Few thought McCarthyism had gotten out of hand.)

The pageant showed the founding of our town and how folks lived hand-to-hand
until Henry Ford and the Great War opened Prosperity's war-bond-wings
over Union Carbide and the First National Bank. But the pilgrim generation
inside Triangle bent their backs, stitched at flimsy thinner than newsprint.
The scrap piles, oil pans, and wicker baskets their circumstance.
Families followed the multiple hearses. One father held a pasteboard script

In his hand: "This is the funeral of Yetta Goldstein." He follows the newsprint
march-map under clouds split in wings. "Heavens Wept" headlines the circumstance.
All this before Commencement or my generation—back when flames wrote the script.

LIPSHITZ & EISENBERG
34
CLOAKS & SUITS
CHIRIN
SUITS
PES & SKIRTS
32
APARTMENTS
TO-LET.
JANITOR
ZUBRINSKY
34
WINDOW
GLASS
SHADES & FRAMES
DONE TO ORDER

TRIANGLE SITE

Asch Building, 1911; Brown Building, 1981

Soaked to skin, look through lens
at Eighth, Ninth, Tenth. So this
is where they worked, I thought

How hot the loft on summer days
and say aloud the layers learned
from photogravure fashion plates:

Pantaloons, petticoats, hour-glass
corsets, one cover called a camisole.
So many strings! In the spinning

Mills down South, steam looms boomed
and even in Winter children stripped
to their shifts, baby hands slick

On cotton bobbins. The shutter clicks,
a pigeon struts and springs. So this
is where they fell. Or jumped.

Layers billow, catch broken rails,
like sails slap on light posts or
pile high on iron fence spears

Where like a little boat, one
pierced shoe holds a paper rose
stem up.

SEAR

July 1982

Always adding. Revising this manuscript.
I plant *direct quotations* on the page,
arranging line-breaks, versification.

Newspaper files: Frances Perkins speaks
from the street, *I felt I must sear it
not only on my mind but on my heart
forever.* One mother, *When will it be
safe to earn our bread?* Their words.
Yet some call that schmaltz, soap-opera-

Sentiment, Victorian melodrama. Riding
the subway, smoke fizzes in my ears and
in my room, electric heater coils glow
*C*s and *O*s in the box. To write about *them*
yet not interfere, although I'm told
a poet's task is to create a little world.

A testimony: Two tried to stay together
on the ledge, but suddenly one twisted
and plunged, a burning bundle. The other
looked ahead, arms straight out, speaking
and shouting *as if addressing an invisible
audience.* She gestured an embrace then

Jumped. Her name was Sally
Weintraub. She lived
on Henry Street.

Rend your hearts, and
not your garments.

—Joel 2:13

THE DAY WHEN MOUNTAINS MOVED

Yosano Akiko, 1911

The mountain-moving day is coming,
I say so yet others doubt.
Only a while the mountain sleeps.
In the past
All mountains moved in fire,
Yet you may not believe it.
Oh man, this alone believe,
All sleeping women now will
awake and move.

SOURCES

Elson, Hilbert. "Triangle Shirtwaist Factory Fire Recalled: Improved Labor Laws Result from Triangle Fire Fifty Years Ago." *NY State Department of Labor Industrial Bulletin* 40 (Mar. 1961): 2–7.

Holy Bible, King James Version. Cleveland and New York: The World Publishing Company, 1951.

Howe, Irving, and Kenneth Libo. *How We Lived: A Documentary History of Jews in America, 1880-1930.* New York: Richard Marek Publishers, 1979.

Kheel Center, Cornell University. *The 1911 Triangle Factory Fire.* Last modified January 2011. http://www.ilr.cornell.edu/index.html.

Kuniczak, W. S. *My Name Is Million: An Illustrated History of the Poles in America.* New York: Doubleday, 1978.

McFarlane, Arthur E. "Fire and the Skyscraper: The Problem of Protecting Workers in New York's Tower Factories." *McClure's Magazine*, 37.5 (Sept. 1911): 467-483.

Militz, Annie Rix. *Spiritual Housekeeping: A Study in Concentration in the Busy Life.* Los Angeles, CA: Master Mind Publishing, 1910.

O'Sullivan, Judith, and Rosemary Gallick. *Workers and Allies: Female Participation in the American Trade Union Movement 1824-1976.* Washington, D.C.: Smithsonian Institution Traveling Exhibition Service, 1975.

Saperstein, Saundra. "Reliving Pain." *Washington Post*, February 1, 1979, C1.

Schneiderman, Rose, and Lucy Goldthwaite. *All for One.* New York: P. S. Ericksson, 1967.

Stein, Leon. *The Triangle Fire.* Philadelphia: J. B. Lippincott, 1962.

Stein, Leon, ed. *Out of the Sweatshop: The Struggle for Industrial Democracy.* New York: Quadrangle/ New York Times Book Co., 1977.

Von Drehle, David. *Triangle: The Fire that Changed America.* New York: Grove P, 2003.

Wertheimer, Barbara. *We Were There: The Story of Working Women in America.* New York: Pantheon, 1977.

ILLUSTRATIONS

Page 11: [*Women Garment Workers Assemble with a Few Men for a Group Portrait*], ca. 1900 (Courtesy of the ILGWU Archives, ILR School, Kheel Center, Cornell University)

Page 17: *Hester Street, New York City*, ca. 1890 (Courtesy of the Library of Congress, Prints and Photographs Division, #LC-USZ62-12528)

Page 22: [*Dead Workers on Sidewalk with Policemen and Others Looking Upward*], ca. 1911 (Courtesy of Brown Brothers, Inc.)

Page 30: [*Flower-Laden Carriage in Silent Procession for Unidentified Victims*], ca. 1911 (Courtesy of the ILGWU Archives, ILR School, Kheel Center, Cornell University)

Page 32: *Trade Union Procession for Fire Victims*, ca. 1911 (Courtesy of the Library of Congress, Prints and Photographs Division, #LC-USZ62-83858)

Page 35: *Garment Girls, June 1911*, ca. 1911 (Courtesy of Ms. Florence Leebov, Pittsburgh, PA)

Page 41: *Shirtwaist Strikers, New York*, ca. 1910 (Courtesy of the Library of Congress, Prints and Photographs Division, #LC-USZ62-51003)

Page 46: *Jews Praying on Williamsburg Bridge, New York City, on New Year's Day*, ca. 1909 (Courtesy of the Library of Congress, Prints and Photographs Division, #LC-USZ62-99960)

Page 53: *Lipshitz & Eisenberg*, date unknown (Courtesy of the Library of Congress)

Essays:

Still Confronting the Great Divide

A Poetics Statement

Summoning the Shade: Poetry as Vocation, Advocation, and Evocation[1]

by Chris Llewellyn

From about fifteen years ago, I frequently had the feeling of rapidly aging while not getting any closer to being a real poet. I was considering revisiting Rilke's *Letters to a Young Poet* when I returned to the "R"s of the public library shelves and instead picked up *The Life of Poetry*. This was to be my relief and recognition. Relief because my poetry journey was affirmed, and recognition because my poetry and politics were compatible with Rukeyser's. Always forceful and never forcing, her words continue to clarify my poetry.

Vocation

While I look at Rukeyser's poetry as vocation, I take the term from the Latin *vocare*, which is a call or summons to a state of action or to the religious life or to regular employment.

I'm remembering how the artist-heroine of Chekhov's "The Seagull" passionately proclaims, "When I think of my vocation I am no longer afraid of life." When I think of Rukeyser's vocation, I am less afraid of my life.

My earliest poems depict the workplaces and workers of childhood memories. In my hometown of Fostoria, Ohio, our livelihoods were dependent on the Union Carbide and auto-parts plants (to this day I know my subjects pick me and not the reverse), but it wasn't until after that first decade of poems that I learned that a poetry of tools, tasks, job conditions, and relationships has a name: labor poetry. After a poetry reading (*Fragments from the Fire: The Triangle Shirtwaist Company Fire of March 25, 1911*), I was approached by Donald Spatz, an AFL-CIO union official representing cement workers, who asked if I could write poems about the Hawk's Nest

---

[1] "Summoning the Shade: Poetry as Vocation, Advocation, and Evocation" was initially published in hardcover format in *"How Shall We Tell Each Other of the Poet?": The Life and Writing of Muriel Rukeyser*, edited by Anne F. Herzog and Janet E. Kaufman, in 1999 by St. Martin's Press and again in 2001 by Palgrave. This essay has been reproduced with permission of Palgrave Macmillan.

Tunnel tragedy. Exploring his idea, I discovered Rukeyser's outstanding labor-poetry sequence, "The Book of the Dead," researched the history of the tunnel, and studied the poems.

Not only the poems about Triangle Shirtwaist, but most of my work I call political, although I use the term close to its origin, i.e., the polis or city-state. Poems that are political address those social and economic concerns and conditions that affect groups of the populace. So I was particularly affirmed and instructed by "The Book of the Dead," the first sequence of political poems with personal content in *U.S. 1* ("Night Music" and "Two Voyages," the second and third sequences, are largely personal poems with social content).

In Rukeyser, I see personal and political intersections in the way events initially external to the poet's personal life (the Hawks Nest Tunnel and other subjects) became absorbed and then expressed by her reportage (social data in dramatic design) and by her poetic-dialectic (my term). As a political science student, I had read the work of Marx and Engels and was influenced by feminist writings such as Shulamith Firestone's *The Dialectic of Sex* (1970). "The Book of the Dead" and others of Rukeyser's poems display a scaffolding of the stages of dialectic materialism: thesis, antithesis, and synthesis. Rukeyser demonstrates and promotes an imagination that sees the unity within opposites and the solutions within contradictions.

Because it investigates relationships in terms of the powerful (again Union Carbide), the powerless, and the empowerment of the powerless, I find "The Book of the Dead" in particular to be a program for social reform. Her voice as poet-narrator, reporter, and witness in this sequence also best represents the state and action of her *vocare*.

Yet Rukeyser's importance to our culture is not due to her skills as dialectician, historian, journalist, etc. Rather, her contribution is due to the qualities of her poetic language and to the accessible *vocare* in her poems. She credits her free-verse voice to her apprenticeships with Walt Whitman, John Milton, and writers of the Holy Scriptures. Here is her *vocare* as a call to the religious life. After all, the Bible does take us back over a thousand years and is a source for ideas of the world (or *cosmos*) and how the word (or *logos*) was expressed and understood. For the ancient Greeks, Logos was reason, reason included passion, and reason was the controlling factor in the universe and, according to the dictionary, "the divine wisdom manifest in the creation, government, and redemption of the world and often identified with the second person of the Trinity."

Logos was the subject of poet St. Francis of Assisi when he wrote: "If thy heart were right, then every creature would be to thee a mirror of life and a book of holy doctrine." In Logos each creature is a book or voice: "The heavens declare the glory of God and the firmament showeth his handiwork. Day unto day uttereth speech, and night unto night showeth knowledge. There is no speech nor language where their voice is not heard" (Psalm 19). Rukeyser acknowledged the scriptures in her *vocare* when she stated, "We are talking about the endless quarrel between the establishment and the prophets, and I hope to be forever on the side of the prophets."

William Blake, George Eliot, Hart Crane, and Jean Toomer come to mind as other poet-prophets who have explored and explained ways the machine age has affected poetic subjects and language. When the Industrial Revolution began in England (c. 1760), machines began replacing hand tools, and huge industrial and social changes arose in the places Blake would describe as "dark satanic mills." Now, as the twenty-first century begins, instead of a respect for Logos, instead of serving humankind, our machine age has high-tech and consumer language that is not held accountable. While Logos was revealing, this language is concealing. "Artificial coloring and flavoring" are listed as food ingredients, and nuclear-warhead missiles are named "peacemaker." Rukeyser's "Poem White Page White Page Poem" summarizes how we as poets predate and postdate the Industrial Revolution. With its breaking waves and standing light, the poem exemplifies Logos:

> Poem   white page   white page   poem
> something is streaming out of a body in waves
> something is beginning from the fingertips[2]

And this is one of several of Rukeyser's poems which affirm the Poet as an embodiment of the raw materials, labor, tools, and tasks, as well as the finished article of poetry.

Advocation

Advocacy (from the Latin *advocare*) is the practice of those who summon and plead the cause of another, and who defend or maintain a cause. Among my pending poetry projects are two biography-based manuscripts, book reviews, and critical papers. Yet I must confess to completing too few poems in my last years. While I long for the space and silence, I don't claim

---

[2]   Rukeyser, Muriel, *A Muriel Rukeyser Reader*, ed. Jan Heller Levi (New York: Norton, 1994), 268.

to have writer's block or a literary "silence." What I have written is dozens of articles, letters, and testimony for public hearings as part of my advocacy work for persons with special needs. Each day I work with my daughter with special needs and am involved in the care of two siblings and partner to my husband who is blind. And then there is preparation for the classes I teach and take. Yet I can turn to Rukeyser as my advocate, teacher, and caretaker. Just as she promises in "Then," she does speak "out of silence" and to my poetic silence.

While I'm surprised to be writing here about my family, advocacy, and poetry work, I am not surprised that it's Rukeyser who provides us with this very forum to talk about the mixedness of our lives. If I can't break through the fear of rejection (among the "resistances" to poetry described in *The Life of Poetry*) to write on this white page and in her presence, then can there be any place to tell my story? Here in my home in Washington, D.C., I am uplifted by her poem "The City of Monuments," in which the "marble men" and buildings are "Split by a tendril of revolt."[3]

I am proud of the way my daughter educates our community about her wholeness. The slogan "it takes a whole village to educate a child" takes on new meaning when reclaimed as "it takes a whole child to educate a village." I find Rukeyser supports such reclamations throughout *The Life of Poetry* and specifically with the adage "All the forms wait for their full language."[4] Despite my advocacy efforts, I have not been able to keep a neighborhood school from being closed or find an employment or housing placement for my daughter. I remember asking a School Board Administrator, a retired high-ranking military officer, if he believed veterans have upheld democracy. And then asking him and others on the panel if they were aware that persons with disabilities are also veterans and that we, their advocates, are veterans as well in the battle against discrimination? And asked if they were aware of how they and their families are just an accident away from having a disability?

Nowadays I see parallels between my advocacy for the inclusion of persons with disabilities and Rukeyser's advocacy for the placement of poetry: "In speaking about poetry, I must say at the beginning that the subject has no acknowledged place in American life today."[5] I am well aware of the resistances, fears, and oversights that work to exclude persons with

---

[3] Rukeyser, Muriel, The Collected Poems of Muriel Rukeyser (New York: McGraw-Hill, 1978), 51.

[4] Rukeyser, Muriel, *The Life of Poetry* (Ashfield, MA: Paris P, 1996), 155.

[5] Rukeyser, *The Life of Poetry*, 5.

disabilities from the "mainstream" of life. I remember Rukeyser advocated to provide a place in poetry for "the lives of Americans who are unpraised and vivid and indicative of my own documents."[6] I remember how she alone kept vigil in the cold and rain outside prison gates in Seoul, how with her physical presence, disabled from stroke, she advocated for the release of Korean poet Kim Chi Ha.

I am writing this on my daughter's birthday, recalling Rukeyser's influences, fishing directives from *The Life of Poetry* to meet my major challenges. I can rely on Rukeyser's *advocare*, the defense of my cause, for she calls out: "you entire / alive among the anti-touch people."[7] Now I'm recalling the birth day. After 30 hours of back labor and within 5 minutes of a prideful Lamaze delivery, the doctor told us ours is a baby with Down syndrome. Weeks later my husband confessed how he wept that day on his long subway ride home, knowing first-hand the resistances our daughter must encounter from those who would judge her based on appearances.

My husband continues to get aggravated with us "sighted folks" who too often don't or won't see. I'm reminded of Rukeyser's refrain, "What do we see? What do we not see?" Stated or implied, it's an ever-present question that summons the reader and listener to a life of advocacy. There's another thing I see in Muriel Rukeyser: where there is no resolution at closure, there is symbolic and often literal transformation or transcendence. When I look at all her advocations and avocations (peace-activist, pilot, photographer, reporter, poet, teacher, biographer, playwright, single parent, etc.), I wonder at her accomplishments. How did she do and be all these?

One thing I do know. She practiced her conviction that truth must be known by the body as well as the intellect. More experiential than empirical, I am reassured when I find her physical presence in her poems and essays.

The Book of Proverbs asks, "A woman of valor who can find?" The great labor organizer Mother Mary Jones was to proclaim, "You can agonize or you can organize." Mother, I want to organize.

For starters, I want *The Life of Poetry* to accompany, if not replace, Rilke's *Letters to a Young Poet* as a standard reference for poetry. It should be on every Introduction to Literature syllabus for students and new poets. First, because unlike Rilke's speaking from Paris prior to two world wars,

---

[6] Ibid., 6.

[7] Rukeyser, *A Muriel Rukeyser Reader*, 251.

Rukeyser is speaking from mid-twentieth century North America about those and subsequent wars, about economic depression, about racial struggles, and about their effects on her life and creativity. Second, because to promote Rilke's standard of solitude yet neglect Rukeyser's head-on-body confrontations does a disservice to those seeking their places in poetry.

Evocation

Evocation, derived from *evocare*, contains a call or summons to re-create imaginatively. I'm always riveted by the *ars poetica* of Whitman, Keats, Shakespeare, and others that directly and presently address the reader. Poems telling us that our eyes and hands, now touching this poem and page, touch live human flesh and not dead paper.

Not just in "Then," but in many of her poems and essays, Rukeyser gives us that *ars poetica* degree of inclusiveness, intimacy, urgency, and presence. Still with us as a presence, she's like a "Shade." (Remember that Dante's shade was Virgil, who acted as spirit-guide to the underworld.) Even today, the Shade approaches…

What do we see? Can we agree that to be a poet is to promote others to use their imagination? To see things in many different ways? To find the common ground? To see new solutions and resolutions? If so, then through our poems and through our teachings of poetry we will empower others to imagine. Alongside she who is caretaker, teacher, and Shade, we will prevail as poets of vocation, advocation, avocation, and evocation.

HISTORICAL CONTEXTS

Sweatshops and Resistance in the 20th and 21st Centuries

by Michelle B. Gaffey

The Triangle Fire remains one of the most politically significant disasters in New York City history and marked a turning point in the US labor movement's struggle for improved working conditions. A year before the fire, in 1909 and 1910, the largest women-led strike in US history—the groundbreaking "Uprising of the Twenty Thousand"—mobilized immigrant women garment workers in New York City. Spearheaded by the International Ladies Garment Workers Union and supported by a number of allies, including the Women's Trade Union League, the strike was significant on a number of levels. As noted in the *Viewers' Guide* to the excellent documentary *Heaven Will Protect the Working Girl*, the strike exposed the "low pay, harsh supervision, and unsafe conditions" that characterized the garment industry in the early 1900s; it countered the assumption that women and girls could not organize to resist poor and unsafe working conditions; it united workers across class, gender, and ethnic lines; and it won important gains from more than three hundred companies in the garment industry.[1]

Despite these victories, however, the largest garment manufacturers, including Triangle, refused to recognize the union and ignored the strikers' demands for improved safety conditions. One year later, 146 garment workers, mostly immigrant women from Eastern Europe, burned, suffocated, or jumped to their deaths during the fire at Triangle. This tragedy galvanized the general public and ignited a social movement in which the people of New York successfully marched, rallied, and lobbied for workplace improvements. In response to their demands, the Factory Investigating Commission and the American Society of Safety Engineers formed in 1911. Later, in the 1930s, the movement won national legislation and reforms under the New Deal that would regulate child labor and ostensibly eliminate US sweatshops by the mid-twentieth century.

---

[1] William Friedheim, Bret Eynon, Joshua Brown, and Andrea Ades Vásquez, "Viewers' Guide to *Heaven Will Protect the Working Girl*" (New York: American Social History Productions, 2007), 10.

Just over a decade after these labor reforms were introduced, however, a series of US foreign policies and trade practices were established that led to the outsourcing of garment work from US factories, the exploitation of workers in the global apparel industry, and the return of the sweatshop to the US garment industry in the late twentieth century. First published in 1987, *Fragments from the Fire*'s poetic content and working-class memories served as a needed intervention into the anti-union policies that arose anew during this time. Its second publication in 1993 coincided with renewed resistance to sweatshop conditions in the US and abroad, and this new edition, published 105 years after the fire, continues to confront the "great divide" between global capital and labor that persists well into this new millennium.

Free Trade and the New Sweatshops

> *Uncle, do not believe gold lies in the street.*
> *This is no golden land.*

—"Dear Uncle Stanislaus"

Although the early 1900s saw "runaway shops" within the US as manufacturers moved their work to southern states to flee unions and labor laws, only after World War II did they begin moving production overseas, taking "advantage of export processing zones in Hong Kong, Taiwan, Korea, and Singapore."[2] The Cold War politics of the 1980s and the expansion of free-trade measures in the early nineties significantly contributed to this offshoring of production. In 1984, for instance, the Caribbean Basin Initiative (CBI) provided economic and military aid and extended trade privileges to Central American and Caribbean countries that the US determined not to be affiliated with left-leaning governments.[3]

---

[2] Eileen Boris, "Consumers of the World, Unite!: Campaigns Against Sweating, Past and Present," in *Sweatshop USA: The American Sweatshop in Historical and Global Perspective*, ed. Daniel E. Bender and Richard A. Greenwald (New York: Routledge, 2003), 212.

[3] The Caribbean Basin Initiative was developed in the context of the labor and land reform movements of the 1970s in Central American and the Caribbean; it stemmed from the Reagan administration's desire to counteract what it perceived to be a dangerous rise in pro-Soviet and Communist activity in Central America and the Caribbean. See also Robert J. S. Ross, *Slaves to Fashion: Poverty and Abuse in the New Sweatshops* (Ann Arbor: University of Michigan Press, 2004)

In 1993, during the Clinton administration, the North American Free Trade Agreement (NAFTA) "gave corporations new legal rights to sue national governments for the enactment of policies that can undermine their profits [and] gave US and Canadian corporations new incentives to re-locate factories to Mexico."[4] Together, the CBI and NAFTA led to a significant increase in the number of garments produced outside the US and directly contributed to the rise of the "new sweatshops" in the eighties and nineties. As American studies professor Andrew Ross has noted, the working conditions of the offshore apparel industry in the Caribbean, Central America, and Mexico offer the "most notorious illustration of a free-trade economy: twenty-hour workdays forced on workers to fill their quotas, widespread sexual harassment, coercive birth control, brutal suppression of labor organization, and starvation wages."[5] This depiction of the "new sweatshop" conditions in the global South reveals just how severely free-trade measures have impacted the lives of workers, especially women and girls in the garment industry.

The gradual decline of labor standards in the late-twentieth-century United States, the extension of global free-trade initiatives, and the rise of weak labor laws in developing nations have all contributed to the reintroduction of sweatshops even inside the United States. Although the mid-twentieth century saw improved working conditions for US garment workers, stemming largely from the mass social movements and legislative reforms in the decades following the Triangle Fire, by the 1980s sweatshops had returned to the US garment industry and have been business as usual ever since. These new sweatshops appear strikingly similar to their nineteenth- and early-twentieth-century predecessors: they are characterized by low or withheld pay, repetitive work, long hours, unpaid and forced overtime, physical abuse, unsafe working conditions, and a subcontracting system of labor.[6] Even the United States General Accounting Office (or GAO, now called the Government Accountability Office), reported in 1994 that

---

4   "Sweatfree FAQs: 'Free Trade' and Sweatshops," *Global Exchange* (website), 2011, http://www.globalexchange.org/fairtrade/sweatfree/faq.

5   Andrew Ross, "The Rise of the Second Anti-Sweatshop Movement," in *Sweatshop USA: The American Sweatshop in Historical and Global Perspective*, ed. Daniel E. Bender and Richard A. Greenwald (New York: Routledge, 2003), 233.

6   A number of explanations of subcontracting in the garment industry are available. Of note are John Commons's 1901 piece "The Sweating System," in *Out of the Sweatshop: The Struggle for Industrial Democracy*, ed. Leon Stein (New York: Quadrangle/New York Times Book Co., 1977), chapter one of Ross's *Slaves to Fashion*, and Nancy Green's "Fashion, Flexible Specialization, and the Sweatshop: A Historical Problem," in Bender and Greenwald, eds., *Sweatshop USA*. A cinematic illustration of the subcontracting system at work can be found in the 2005 documentary *China Blue*.

"sweatshop working conditions remain a major problem in the US garment industry" and that "the description of today's sweatshops differs little from that at the turn of the century."[7]

The Globalized Race to the Bottom

Bent over Singers, their backs to factory windows,
women and children stitch into sunset.

—"The Great Divide"

Despite the undeniable similarities between working conditions in early twentieth-century sweatshops, one major factor distinguishes today's sweatshops: they are now, more than ever, enmeshed in a process of corporate globalization. Today's manufacturers compete globally to produce garments in the least restrictive regulatory environments, a common practice known as the "race to the bottom," a globalized version of the early twentieth century's runaway shop. Thus, in an effort to produce garments that make significant profits for manufacturers—primarily for US and European corporations and brands—manufacturers typically subcontract their work to areas where wages are very low and the right to organize is brutally suppressed, thereby decreasing working and living standards across the globe. This race to the bottom accounts for the 255,000 people who worked in US sweatshops in the year 2000, as well as the millions of women who continue to produce garments in sweatshops in Bangladesh alone.[8]

In 1995 many Americans became familiar with this race to the bottom, as well as the reality of the new sweatshops, because of the discovery of what was dubbed a "slaveshop" in El Monte, California—a case of human trafficking in which "seventy-two Thai [immigrants] bent over machines behind barbed wire producing clothes for Nordstrom, Sears . . . and other brand-name stores."[9] The work of the Institute for Global Labour and Human Rights (formerly known as the National Labor Committee) also contributed greatly to publicizing the realities of sweatshop working

---

[7] Linda G. Morra, "Report, GAO/HEHS-95-29: 'Garment Industry: Efforts to Address the Prevalence and Conditions of Sweatshops,'" (Washington, DC: United States General Accounting Office, 1994), http://www.gao.gov/assets/230/220498.pdf.

[8] Ross, *Slaves to Fashion*, 35.

[9] Boris, "Consumers of the World," 214.

conditions; its executive director Charles Kernaghan made sweatshops a household topic when, in 1996, he publicly exposed talk show host Kathie Lee Gifford for operating a clothing line with garments sewn by young girls and women in Guatemalan sweatshops.

This televised public scrutiny of poor working conditions in the global apparel industry in the 1990s sparked the contemporary anti-sweatshop movement in the US. In fact, the first two publications of Llewellyn's *Fragments from the Fire* coincided not only with the rise of the new American and global sweatshop, but also with the formation of human rights and community organizations, labor unions, activist groups, and arts groups dedicated to raising awareness about and combating sweatshop conditions. Throughout the eighties and nineties, for instance, immigrant women garment workers "were organizing . . . through groups like the New York City's Chinese Staff and Workers Association, *La Mujer Obrera* in Texas and California's Asian Immigrant Women Advocates."[10]

Too, the highly influential student-led anti-sweatshop organization, United Students Against Sweatshops (USAS), initiated its model of worker-consumer solidarity in the late nineties by successfully pressuring university administrations to adopt meaningful codes of conduct that required manufacturers of school apparel to "maintain safe, independently monitored workplaces in which workers were free to organize"; these codes were later amended to require full public disclosure of factory locations in which apparel was made "so students and other researchers could investigate schools' sweatshop problems, and make contact with workers."[11]

And since 1984, the National Garment Workers' Federation of Bangladesh, an independent nationwide federation of garment workers, has been intimately involved with the sustained efforts of garment workers in Bangladesh to organize some of the largest strikes the global apparel industry has ever seen. *Fragments from the Fire*, whose documentary poems gesture toward the need for continued concerted action against sweatshop conditions, thus began circulating throughout the United States during the return of sweatshops *and* resistance against these sweatshops in the US and across the globe.

---

[10] Liza Featherstone, "Students Against Sweatshops: A History," in Bender and Greenwald, eds., *Sweatshop USA*, 250.

[11] Featherstone, "Students Against Sweatshops," 250.

Sweatshops and Factory Fires in the New Millennium

There they are on tops of hundreds of
buildings—structures no different from
the Asch Building and as for lacking
Fire protection, many much worse
than Triangle.

—"Funeral for the Nameless"

This new edition of *Fragments from the Fire* is equally, if not more, relevant since sweatshop conditions still pervade the global apparel industry well into the twenty-first century. In 2003, for instance, the owner of the Daewoosa factory in American Samoa was convicted of human trafficking, a case the US attorney general "described as 'nothing less than modern-day slavery.'"[12] The Institute for Global Labour and Human Rights had exposed the sweatshop conditions at Daewoosa two years earlier, revealing in its investigative reports that garment workers were beaten and starved and that management routinely withheld workers' pay and severely punished those who spoke out against the abuse and labor violations. Likewise, in recent years the Institute has published dozens of reports disclosing the repeated sexual assault and rape of guest workers sewing clothing for major US corporations at the Classic Factory in Jordan, violations that took place "in broad daylight under the US-Jordan Free Trade Agreement."[13]

Read in this context, the poems in this book generalize the experiences of garment workers in 1911 to move readers to question the system of profit and exploitation that has led to the ubiquity of sweatshop conditions in the global apparel industry. Contemporary readers might identify with the Sophies and Dellas of garment factories around the world who work in "modern-day Triangles":

---

[12] David Fickling, "Misery of Rag-Trade Slaves in America's Pacific Outpost: Workers in Samoan Sweatshop Beaten and Starved," *Guardian*, February 28, 2003, http://www.guardian.co.uk/world/2003/mar/01/usa.globalisation.

[13] "Alerts: 'Another Young Woman Disappeared at the Classic Factory in Jordan Sewing Jeans for Wal-Mart,'" *Institute for Global Labour and Human Rights* (website), August 16, 2012, http://www.globallabourrights.org/alerts?id=0394.

- The 283 textile workers in Pakistan who, on September 11, 2012, burned and suffocated to death in a factory fire because of locked exit doors, a lack of safety equipment, and inadequate labor laws.[14]

- The 112 workers in Dhaka, Bangladesh who died three months later in the Tazreen Fashions Factory. These women and men were working mandatory overtime shifts in a building with faulty fire extinguishers, no fire escapes, and a locked exit door, causing many workers to jump to their deaths to escape the heat and flames of their burning building. Multiple survivors of this blaze recall being forced to stay at their machines, trapped inside by collapsible gates, which managers pulled down to keep workers focused on production even while the fire alarms sounded.[15]

- The 1,100 Bangladeshi garment workers who were crushed to death on April 24, 2013, when the illegally-constructed Rana Plaza collapsed near Dhaka. At this factory, workers were threatened and ordered by management to continue with their work even though police had ordered an evacuation a day earlier because the building displayed obvious signs of significant structural damage.[16]

As it imagines the final moments of Sophie Salemi and Della Costello (Josie Del Castillo) in "March 25, 1911," *Fragments from the Fire* invites us to, in the words of Karen Kovacik, "indict [the] predatory, profit-driven" system of production that ultimately led to the fire at Triangle,[17] the same production system that led to the return of the sweatshop and workplace disasters in the late twentieth and early twenty-first centuries.

These poems further demand that we consider how the deregulation of business even inside the US—at both the state and national levels—has led to a decrease in funding for the agencies that are supposed to investigate workplaces for safety violations. This lack of resources has contributed to

---

[14] Adil Jawad and Sebastian Abbot, "Pakistan Factory Fires Kill Nearly 300 in Karachi," *Huffington Post*, September 12, 2012, http://www.huffingtonpost.com/2012/09/12/pakistan-factory-fires-2012_n_1875984.html.

[15] Charles Kernaghan, "Alerts: 'Criminal Negligence Leads to Tragedy at the Tazreen Fashion Factory in Bangladesh,'" *Institute for Global Labour and Human Rights* (website), November 27, 2012, http://www.globallabourrights.org/alerts?id=0401.

[16] Chris Blake and Farid Hossain, "Bangladesh Building Collapse: Protesters Demand Worker Safety as Death Toll Tops 400," *Huffington Post*, May 1, 2013, http://www.huffingtonpost.com/2013/05/01/bangladesh-building-collapse-death-toll_n_3191087.html.

[17] Karen Kovacik, "Words of Fire for Our Generation: Contemporary Working-Class Poets on the Triangle Fire," *Women's Studies Quarterly* 26:1/2 (1998), 147.

US factory fires outside the garment industry as well. In 1991, for instance, twenty-five workers were killed and another fifty-four were injured at the Imperial Foods Processing Plant in Hamlet, North Carolina. Investigations following the fire revealed that one exit had been blocked by a trailer and another had been locked from the outside, preventing many employees from escaping the deadly smoke.[18] In the plant's eleven years of operation, the North Carolina Department of Occupational Safety and Health Administration (OSHA) had never inspected the factory; reports later indicated that "workers inside the Hamlet Plant were afraid to say anything about safety conditions due to fear of being fired."[19]

More recently, in April 2013, a fire and explosion at a fertilizer plant in West, Texas claimed fifteen lives, injured hundreds of people, and devastated an entire community in a disaster that, according to the United States Chemical Safety and Hazard Investigation Board (CSB), "was preventable" and "should never have occurred."[20] As Texas-based journalist and labor activist Ryan Hill reported a day after the explosion, "The company checked 'no' under fire and explosive risks" even though no sprinkler or fire detection systems were installed in the building, and "speculated that 'the worst possible [accident] scenario . . . would be a 10-minute release of ammonia gas that would kill or injure no one.'"[21] Based on the violent reality of the actual accident, Hill aptly concludes that "we can only take the bosses at their word at our own risk."[22]

---

[18] Department of Homeland Security/United States Fire Administration National Fire Data Center, *Chicken Processing Plant Fires: Hamlet, North Carolina and North Little Rock, Arkansas, USFA-TR-057*, June/September 1991, 4, http://www.usfa.fema.gov/downloads/pdf/publications/tr-057.pdf.

[19] Department of Homeland Security/United States Fire Administration National Fire Data Center, *Chicken Processing Plant Fires*, 11.

[20] Rafael Moure-Eraso and Johnnie Banks, "Statement by CSB," News Conference, April 22, 2014, 1, http://www.csb.gov/assets/1/16/Statement_-_News_Conference_(Final).pdf.

[21] Ryan Hill, "On the Tragic Plant Explosion in West, Texas," *Solidarity* (website), April 18, 2013, http://www.solidarity-us.org/site/node/3837.

[22] Hill, "On the Tragic Plant Explosion," *Solidarity* (website).

Collective Resistance and Global Solidarity

Where are the words of fire for my generation?

—"Stadium Sestina"

Perhaps even more importantly, though, readers of Llewellyn's finely crafted political poems might be moved to consider the mass demonstrations and publicity campaigns that have demanded stronger labor and safety laws and improved working conditions throughout the past century. In doing so, readers will likely make connections between exploitation *and* resistance across time and geographic location, between the social movement following the Triangle Fire of 1911 and the "Wisconsin Uprising" a hundred years later, in which thousands of people marched on their state capitol after the governor took measures to curtail collective bargaining rights, or between the first-ever worker-led walkouts from US Walmarts on "Black Friday" in 2012 and the fifteen-thousand-strong protest near Dhaka a week later, organized after the Tazreen Fashions Factory workers died while sewing products for major US retailers, including Walmart.

In making such connections, readers will discover significant victories and organizing possibilities. In 2009, for example, Bangladeshi garment workers at the R. L. Denim Factory won improved working and safety conditions, paid maternity leave, overtime pay, and the right to work toward forming an independent union. This victory was made possible by the courageous grassroots organizing efforts of the workers at R. L. Denim and through the solidarity work of unions and human rights organizations on several continents around the world. As the Institute for Global Labour and Human Rights has noted:

> This was international solidarity at its best... In the U.S., the United Steelworkers union played a major role, coordinating with Workers Uniting and the UNITE union in the United Kingdom and the *Verdi* union in Germany. The German Clean Clothes Campaign and the Romero Christian Initiative [also] played key roles.[23]

---

[23] "Alerts: 'Unprecedented Victory for Workers across the Developing World,'" *Institute for Global Labour and Human Rights* (website), June 19, 2009, http://www.globallabourrights. org/alerts?id=0040.

This unprecedented victory underscores the importance of organizing against sweatshops—a global problem—through international solidarity.

Given this historical context, the poems and photographs within this book provide an "antidote," as Janet Zandy has suggested, to the "aphasia caused by class hegemony over culture,"[24] as *Fragments* reminds us that we must *remember* the past, particularly through narratives by working people and about workers' struggles, if we are *to win* in the present. These poems—and the history and memories they evoke—empower us to imagine organizing possibilities that are guided by a vision of a new world order in which the global sweatshop is a relic of the past.

---

[24] Janet Zandy, "Fire Poetry on the Triangle Shirtwaist Company Fire of March 25, 1911," *College Literature* 24: 3 (1997), 51.

Coda:

Remembering those who Perished in the Fire

Victims List

Names and Ages of the 146 Lives Lost in the Triangle Fire of March 25, 1911

Courtesy of the Kheel Center, Cornell University

Adler, Lizzie, 24

Altman, Anna, 16

Ardito, Annina, 25

Bassino, Rose, 31

Benanti, Vincenza, 22

Berger, Yetta, 18

Bernstein, Essie, 19

Bernstein, Jacob, 38

Bernstein, Morris, 19

Billota, Vincenza, 16

Binowitz, Abraham, 30

Birman, Gussie, 22

Brenman, Rosie, 23

Brenman, Sarah, 17

Brodsky, Ida, 15

Brodsky, Sarah, 21

Brucks, Ada, 18

Brunetti, Laura, 17

Cammarata, Josephine, 17

Caputo, Francesca, 17

Carlisi, Josephine, 31

Caruso, Albina, 20

Ciminello, Annie, 36

Cirrito, Rosina, 18

Cohen, Anna, 25

Colletti, Annie, 30

Cooper, Sarah, 16

Cordiano , Michelina, 25

Dashefsky, Bessie, 25

Del Castillo, Josie, 21

Dockman, Clara, 19

Donick, Kalman, 24

Driansky, Nettie, 21

Eisenberg, Celia, 17

Evans, Dora, 18

Feibisch, Rebecca, 20

Fichtenholtz, Yetta, 18

Fitze, Daisy Lopez, 26

Floresta, Mary, 26

Florin, Max, 23

Franco, Jenne, 16

Friedman, Rose, 18

Gerjuoy, Diana, 18

Gerstein, Molly, 17

Giannattasio, Catherine, 22

Gitlin, Celia, 17

Goldstein, Esther, 20

Goldstein, Lena, 22

Goldstein, Mary, 18

Goldstein, Yetta, 20

Grasso, Rosie, 16

Greb, Bertha, 25

Grossman, Rachel, 18

Herman, Mary, 40

Hochfeld, Esther, 21

Hollander, Fannie, 18

Horowitz, Pauline, 19

Jukofsky, Ida, 19

Kanowitz, Ida, 18

Kaplan, Tessie, 18

Kessler, Beckie, 19

Klein, Jacob, 23

Koppelman, Beckie, 16

Kula, Bertha, 19

Kupferschmidt, Tillie, 16

Kurtz, Benjamin, 19

L'Abbate, Annie, 16

Lansner, Fannie, 21

Lauletti, Maria Giuseppa, 33

Lederman, Jennie, 21

Lehrer, Max, 18

Lehrer, Sam, 19

Leone, Kate, 14

Leventhal, Mary, 22

Levin, Jennie, 19

Levine, Pauline, 19

Liebowitz, Nettie, 23

Liermark, Rose, 19

Maiale, Bettina, 18

Maiale, Frances, 21

Maltese, Catherine, 39

Maltese, Lucia, 20

Maltese, Rosaria, 14

Manaria, Maria, 27

Mankofsky, Rose, 22

Mehl, Rose, 15

Meyers, Yetta, 19

Midolo, Gaetana, 16

Miller, Annie, 16

Neubauer, Beckie, 19

Nicholas, Annie, 18

Nicolosi, Michelina, 21

Nussbaum, Sadie, 18

Oberstein, Julia, 19

Oringer, Rose, 19

Ostrovsky , Beckie, 20

Pack, Annie, 18

Panno, Provindenza, 43

Pasqualicchio, Antonietta, 16

Pearl, Ida, 20

Pildescu, Jennie, 18

Pinelli, Vincenza, 30

Prato, Emilia, 21

Prestifilippo, Concetta, 22

Reines, Beckie, 18

Rosen (Loeb), Louis, 33

Rosen, Fannie, 21

Rosen, Israel, 17

Rosen, Julia, 35

Rosenbaum, Yetta, 22

Rosenberg, Jennie, 21

Rosenfeld, Gussie, 22

Rothstein, Emma, 22

Rotner, Theodore, 22

Sabasowitz, Sarah, 17

Salemi, Santina, 24

Saracino, Sarafina, 25

Saracino, Teresina, 20

Schiffman, Gussie, 18

Schmidt, Theresa, 32

Schneider, Ethel, 20

Schochet, Violet, 21

Schpunt, Golda, 19

Schwartz, Margaret, 24

Seltzer, Jacob, 33

Shapiro, Rosie, 17

Sklover, Ben, 25

Sorkin, Rose, 18

Starr, Annie, 30

Stein, Jennie, 18

Stellino, Jennie, 16

Stiglitz, Jennie, 22

Taback, Sam, 20

Terranova, Clotilde, 22

Tortorelli, Isabella, 17

Utal, Meyer, 23

Uzzo, Catherine, 22

Velakofsky, Frieda, 20

Viviano, Bessie, 15

Weiner, Rosie, 20

Weintraub, Sarah, 17

Weisner, Tessie, 21

Welfowitz, Dora, 21

Wendroff, Bertha, 18

Wilson, Joseph, 22

Wisotsky, Sonia, 17

Reflections

Reflections

Reflections

Reflections

Reflections

Reflections

9 781939 044037